You're God's Gift to Teachers

Passages of Biblical
Encouragement for Teachers

John Marder

Outskirts Press, Inc.
Denver, Colorado

Outskirts Press, Inc.
http://www.outskirtspress.com

ISBN: 978-1-4327-3699-6

Library of Congress Control Number: 2008940470

Outskirts Press and the "OP" logo are trademarks belonging to Outskirts Press, Inc.

PRINTED IN THE UNITED STATES OF AMERICA

DEDICATION

To Samantha and Candy for all of the hard work
and love you give to your students.
I'm in awe of how important your jobs are,
and what a great job you are doing.

TABLE OF TOPICS

I

INTRODUCTION

I have been surrounded by teachers my whole life. Dad was a teacher, and later a headmaster for a private school in Orange County, California. My grandmother was a teacher. My uncle was a professor. Mom was a teacher. My stepmother was a teacher. My only sister is a teacher. My wife is a teacher. And as of last year, now my daughter is a teacher. How I caught the bug to go into the finance world is anybody's guess.

But, I have always respected what these and other teachers do, day in and day out. I think we all recognize how important their role is, but may not recognize how difficult this job is. Despite the fact that teachers mostly like what they do, it doesn't mean that the struggles don't exist. Just think of it – each teacher is almost like a CEO of a company. They need to deal with the board of directors (school administration), stockholders (parents), employees (students), and operations (teaching)! But perhaps the

I

setting is even more difficult than a CEO, since students are matters of the heart, and even more precious than money.

Every day, teachers must make many important decisions. In most cases, they have received significant training to assist them in making decisions. But teachers know every case is a little different.

Where do you find the answers? How do you deal with a bad day? Or a bad parent meeting? Or a slow learner? A frustrated student? How do you respond to a problem with the administration? How do you prevent from getting burned out? Having been around teachers my whole life, I have heard stories about many of these issues.

Over the years, I began to notice that God has provided much guidance and inspiration for teachers throughout the bible. At a church retreat, I was inspired to share my observations through this little book. This book contains many nuggets of God's stories and examples for today's teacher. The format intentionally emphasizes the biblical

I

passage, because it is this, and not my comments, that are the inspired word of God. I am only here to provide a little bit of context. In case these passages prompt some follow-up, I give you some space to make some notes, specific applications, or reminder to pray for someone.

Teachers are perhaps most uniquely positioned to make changes in the life of a child. My hope is that in some small way, this book can be a resource to help change a life, either yours or your students. I invite you to notice God's gifts for you in your work. I know this will also spill over into your life and relationships outside of work. But I'm going to sit back and let God do the work from here.

Remember:

Each of you has received a gift to use to serve others. Be good servants of God's various gifts of grace.

1 Peter 4:10 NCV

YOU'RE GOD'S GIFT TO TEACHERS

Assembled and "Narrated"

By

John F. Marder

ADVERSITY
(GROWING THROUGH)

Dear brothers and sisters, when troubles come your way, consider it an opportunity for great joy. For you know that when your faith is tested, your endurance has a chance to grow.
So let it grow, for when your endurance is fully developed, you will be perfect and complete, needing nothing.

James 1: 2 NLT

Ever have a bad day? Of course, you have. Even in a bad day, God has a gift for you. This passage gives a clue about the "benefits" of adversity. Trouble builds character. While nobody is out looking for trouble, can you imagine how little strength of character you would have if you never faced any challenges? Teachers face plenty of these character-builders.

NOTES/THOUGHTS/PRAYERS

ADVERSITY
(OVERCOMING)

But even if you do suffer for doing what is right, you are blessed. Do not fear what they fear, and do not be intimidated.

1 Peter 3:14 NRSV

God's encouragement here is to stay the course when you know what you are doing is right. Hold to the high ground in all your teaching challenges.

Notes/Thoughts/Prayers

_____

_____

_____

_____

_____

_____

_____

_____

_____

_____

ADVICE
(SEEKING)

Without counsel, plans go wrong, but with many advisers they succeed.

Proverbs 15:22 NRSV

God has dropped many gems into Proverbs, written by King Solomon. Solomon is widely recognized as one of the wisest men in history. Here he counsels that, while you make the ultimate decision, it is wise to seek input from your advisers. This can help keep your plans from going wrong.

NOTES/THOUGHTS/PRAYERS

ADVICE
(SHARING)

Fools are headstrong and do what they like; wise people take advice.

Proverbs 12:15 Message

Here is a little more "in your face" reminder about seeking advice. God has given you a gift of teaching, but also a gift to remind you that even the good teachers get better by consulting with other good teachers. Also, enjoy sharing your gifts with other teachers in the interest of benefiting their students too.

NOTES/THOUGHTS/PRAYERS

_____

_____

_____

_____

_____

_____

_____

_____

_____

ANGER
(RESPONDING TO)

A soft answer turns away wrath, but a harsh word stirs up anger.

Proverbs 15:1 NKJV

Teachers are constantly dealing with students, parents, administration and other teachers. It's bound to happen that someone says something wrong, and things escalate. God's gift is to caution about getting angry, and provide guidance in how to deal with it (a "soft answer").

NOTES/THOUGHTS/PRAYERS

ANGER
(SLOW TO)

Don't become angry quickly, because getting angry is foolish.

Ecclesiastes 7: 9 NCV

Easier said than done - don't be quick to anger. Teachers have a fast-paced day, and need to deal with things quickly as they come along. More than likely, this will just happen without you knowing it. But God's reminder is a good one. It's not the right thing to do, and it could have a long term impact on one of your key relationships, whether it is a parent, student or another teacher.

NOTES/THOUGHTS/PRAYERS

_____

_____

_____

_____

_____

_____

_____

_____

_____

_____

ANGER
(LET GO OF)

You shall not take vengeance or bear any grudge against the sons of your own people, but you shall love your neighbor as yourself: I am the Lord.

Leviticus 19:18 RSV

Don't allow a tough parent or a difficult administrator make you take it to the next level, and try to get back at them. God reminds you to just let it go, and handle it some other way. Your response will blow them away!

NOTES/THOUGHTS/PRAYERS

_____

_____

_____

_____

_____

_____

_____

_____

B

BALANCE IN LIFE

For everything there is a season, a time for every activity under heaven.
A time to be born and a time to die.
A time to plant and a time to harvest.
A time to kill and a time to heal.
A time to tear down and a time to build up.
A time to cry and a time to laugh.
A time to grieve and a time to dance.

Ecclesiastes 3: 1-4 NLT

This passage was made famous in the Byrd's song *Turn! Turn! Turn!* from the 1960's. It continues on for several more verses all of which describe the importance of balance in life. God's gift to teachers here is the reminder to put balance in your lives. No doubt, many teachers take their work home in one form or another: homework grading, the problem student, the nasty comment from someone. Remember to make time for everyone and everything in your life. Don't burn out.

B

NOTES/THOUGHTS/PRAYERS

_____

_____

_____

_____

_____

_____

_____

_____

_____

B

BLESSINGS

"May the Lord bless you and keep you. May the Lord show you his kindness and have mercy on you. May the Lord watch over you and give you peace."

Number 6: 24 NCV

"I leave you peace; my peace I give you. I do not give it to you as the world does. So don't let your hearts be troubled or afraid.

John 14: 27 NCV

God provides the gift of many blessings throughout the Bible. May these blessings give you comfort and inspiration.

B

NOTES/THOUGHTS/PRAYERS

_____

_____

_____

_____

_____

_____

_____

_____

C

CARING
(WORKS)

"Which one of you, having a hundred sheep and losing one of them, does
not leave the ninety-nine in the wilderness and go after the one
that is lost until he finds it?
When he has found it, he lays it on his shoulders and rejoices.
And when he comes home,
he calls together his friends and neighbors,
saying to them,
'Rejoice with me, for I have found my sheep that was lost.' "

Luke 15:4-6 NRSV

As a teacher, you can often spend a disproportionate amount of time with your slower students. God's word provides encouragement for that extra effort when they finally "get it".

NOTES/THOUGHTS/PRAYERS

_____

_____

_____

_____

_____

_____

_____

_____

C

COMFORT
(PASS IT ALONG)

He comforts us in all our troubles so that we can comfort others.
When they are troubled,
we will be able to give them the same comfort God has given us.

2 Corinthians 1:4 NLT

This beautiful passage is a fantastic gift from you to others. For believers in God, you can share the comfort you receive from him with others. Pass on that same peace and comfort to your students, parents, co-workers…and everyone else.

NOTES/THOUGHTS/PRAYERS

_____

_____

_____

_____

_____

_____

_____

_____

_____

C

CONFIDENCE
(WORKS)

She is clothed with strength and dignity,
and she laughs without fear of the future.
When she speaks, her words are wise,
and she gives instructions with kindness.

Proverbs 31:25-26 NLT

For the ladies, inserted at the very end of Proverbs, God provides the picture of a beautifully confident, "noble woman". Strength. Dignity. Fearless. Wise. Teaches with kindness. This vision is a great way to start each school day, and should make facing the challenges of a typical teacher's day a breeze. For a complete description of this woman, read Proverbs 31 starting at verse 10.

NOTES/THOUGHTS/PRAYERS

_____

_____

_____

_____

_____

_____

_____

_____

C

CONVICTION
(COURAGE OF YOUR)

*So let us not grow weary in doing what is right, for we will reap at
harvest time, if we do not give up.*

Galatians 6:9 NRSV

The bible encourages us to keep doing what is right and not
give up. How rewarding is it to see progress in a student
and family that you thought would never make it, or even
one that fought you all the way. Keep at it.

NOTES/THOUGHTS/PRAYERS

_____

_____

_____

_____

_____

_____

_____

_____

C

COURAGE
(WITH LOVE)

*For God has not given us a spirit of fear and timidity,
but of power, love, and self-discipline.*

2 Timothy 1:7 NLT

*But as for you, be strong and courageous,
for your work will be rewarded.*

2 Chronicles 15:7 NLT

Who needs the benefit of little extra confidence more than teachers on the first day of school, or during parent conference week? These are a reminder of how to approach your role - firmness of power and self-discipline, but always with love.

NOTES/THOUGHTS/PRAYERS

_____

_____

_____

_____

_____

_____

_____

_____

C

COURAGE
(EVERYDAY)

*Remember that I commanded you to be strong and brave. Don't be
afraid, because the Lord your God will be with you everywhere you go.*

Joshua 1:9 NCV

Teachers get a lot of different things thrown at them from a
lot of different angles. The more years you teach, the more
you are prepared. But still, whether you are new or
experienced, there is bound to be something you would
prefer not to face. For these situations, God gives the gift of
his courage to get you through.

NOTES/THOUGHTS/PRAYERS

_____

_____

_____

_____

_____

_____

_____

_____

D

DISABILITIES
(HELPING THOSE WITH)

That evening a lot of demon-afflicted people were brought to him. He relieved the inwardly tormented. He cured the bodily ill. He fulfilled Isaiah's well-know sermon: "He took our illnesses, He carried our diseases."

Matthew 8:16-17 Message

Jesus did not avoid people with disabilities; he helped them. This is easier said than done for today's busy teacher. It is difficult for us to imagine how much longer it takes a disabled student to get ready for school, or perform a task, or know they can't do something all the other students *can* do. God's gift of additional patience for teachers to help such children is needed here.

D

NOTES/THOUGHTS/PRAYERS

_____

_____

_____

_____

_____

_____

_____

_____

D

DISABILITIES

Then he turned to his host. "The next time you put on a dinner, don't just invite your friends and family and rich neighbors, the kind of people who will return the favor. Invite some people who never get invited out, the misfits from the wrong side of the tracks. You'll be – and experience - a blessing. They won't be able to return the favor, but the favor will be returned – oh, and how it will be returned!-at the resurrection of God's people."

Luke 14:12-14 Message

This passage reminds us of the blessings a teacher receives when offering a kind hand or comment, or additional help for a slow learner or disabled person. Using the example of a dinner instead of a classroom, Jesus encourages us to remember the "misfits", and invite them to be with you, so you can use your gifts to help them learn.

D

NOTES/THOUGHTS/PRAYERS

_____

_____

_____

_____

_____

_____

_____

_____

D

DISCIPLINE
(IMPORTANCE OF)

No discipline is enjoyable while it is happening—it's painful! But afterward there will be a peaceful harvest of right living for those who are trained in this way.

Hebrew 12:11 NLT

This is encouragement from God that when all is said and done, discipline turns out solid citizens. You use discipline with your students, but also find yourself coaching parents in their efforts for the benefit of the child. Teachers need this encouragement along the way because discipline frankly can be a big challenge. Even more frustrating, the positive outcome may not be evident for years, and you might never even see the results. This passage, and many others throughout the bible, provides the assurance that you are on the right course.

D

NOTES/THOUGHTS/PRAYERS

_____

_____

_____

_____

_____

_____

_____

_____

_____

D

DISCIPLINE
(IS IMPORTANT)

Those who spare the rod of discipline hate their children. Those who love their children care enough to discipline them.

Proverbs 13:24 NLT

Correct your children, and you will be proud; they will give you satisfaction.

Proverbs 29:17 NCV

Pass this on to your parents. In the name of love, encourage your parents to help you with this at home. This is one of God's most important instructions to parents that is often misunderstood and ignored. Have a list of resources (such as the book *Dare to Discipline* by James Dobson) for those who don't get it.

D

NOTES/THOUGHTS/PRAYERS

_____

_____

_____

_____

_____

_____

_____

_____

D

DISCIPLINE
(YOUR CHILDREN)

Intelligent children listen to their parents;
foolish children do their own thing.

Proverbs 13:1 Message

This comes right out of the wisdom of King Solomon and his circle of wise men. The "problem student" at school often starts with the "problem child" at home. You need all the help you can get from the home front. This passage isn't as much for a finger-wagging lecture to the child, but more of an advisory to the parent. Parents need to instill this at home over time, and with it will come the desired results.

D

Notes/Thoughts/Prayers

_____

_____

_____

_____

_____

_____

_____

_____

_____

E

EFFORT
(PAYS OFF)

A lazy person will end up poor, but a hard worker will become rich.

Proverbs 10:4 NCV

Many famous people have stated this in one form or another, but God's encouragement here in Proverbs was perhaps the oldest reference to this good advice about the benefits of hard work. "Rich" ness for teachers is likely to be measured in things other than money. Wait until your hard work is rewarded by the return of a student who says "I couldn't have made it through without you".

NOTES/THOUGHTS/PRAYERS

_____

_____

_____

_____

_____

_____

_____

_____

EFFORT
(EXTRA)

In all the work you are doing, work the best you can. Work as if you were doing it for the Lord, not for people.

Colossians 3: 23 NCV

The diligent find freedom in their work; the lazy are oppressed by work.

Proverbs 12:24 Message

And whoever compels you to go one mile, go with him two.

Matthew 5:41 NKJV

Here are three short comments about the benefits of hard work. "Work your best." "Hard workers enjoy their work more." And finally, there is this most famous passage from Matthew's accounts of the days of Christ, still is use every day 20 centuries later - "Go the extra mile". Your extra effort with your students is a gift from God and therefore an expression of love.

NOTES/THOUGHTS/PRAYERS

_____

_____

_____

_____

_____

_____

_____

_____

EMPATHY

By helping each other with your troubles,
you truly obey the law of Christ.

Galatians 6:2 NCV

Everybody runs into troubling times. It's just easier for it to happen to a teacher because your day is so filled with the issues of others, especially your students, parents or other teachers. Come along side someone in need, and you will feel better, maybe now or maybe later.

NOTES/THOUGHTS/PRAYERS

_____

_____

_____

_____

_____

_____

_____

_____

ENCOURAGEMENT
(MOTIVATES)

Fathers, do not aggravate your children, or they will become discouraged.

Colossians 3:21 NLT

God inserts a reminder here, courtesy of Paul's letter to the Colossian church, that children can be easily discouraged. Some students handle frustration better than others, but constant aggravation can really gnaw at kids over time. You are more effective if your students aren't discouraged.

NOTES/THOUGHTS/PRAYERS

_____

_____

_____

_____

_____

_____

_____

_____

E

ENCOURAGEMENT
(PEOPLE RESPOND TO)

When they were discouraged, I smiled at them.
My look of approval was precious to them.

Job 29:24 NLT

When the king smiles, there is life; his favor refreshes like a spring rain.

Proverbs 16:15 NLT

God's gift of a smile to a child can make their day, week or
year. Teachers are in a unique position to affirm children
through a kind word or even just a smile.

NOTES/THOUGHTS/PRAYERS

_____

_____

_____

_____

_____

_____

_____

_____

_____

E

EXCELLENCE

You are the light that gives light to the world. A city that is built on a hill cannot be hidden. And people don't hide a light under a bowl. They put it on a lamp stand so the light shines for all the people in the house. In the same way, you should be a light for other people. Live so that they will see the good things you do and will praise your Father in heaven.

Matthew 5:14-16 NCV

As much as any other profession, teachers bring light to the world through education. Through you, God is giving the gift of learning, but also putting you in a place where parents, children and others can visibly see the good things you do. This is a great gift to you.

Notes/Thoughts/Prayers

_____

_____

_____

_____

_____

_____

_____

F

FAIRNESS
(BRINGS ORDER)

Justice will bring about peace; right will produce calm and security.

Isaiah 32:17 NABWRNT

The gift of justice maintains order in the classroom. Children especially notice differences in treatment and set their limits based on your limits. Making the tough calls with proper consequences makes your classroom easier.

F

NOTES/THOUGHTS/PRAYERS

_____

_____

_____

_____

_____

_____

_____

_____

_____

F

FAIRNESS
(JUDGE WITH)

"This is what the LORD of Heaven's Armies says:
Judge fairly, and show mercy and kindness to one another."

Zechariah 7:19 NLT

Teachers are constantly required to judge their students. In fact, at the end of the term, you have to give each student a grade. The bible always reminds to use kindness and fairness with each of these decisions.

F

NOTES/THOUGHTS/PRAYERS

_____

_____

_____

_____

_____

_____

_____

_____

F

FAITH
(GETS YOU THROUGH)

Now faith is the substance of things hoped for,
the evidence of things not seen.

Hebrews 11:1 KJV

Remember the gift of this simple passage. God gives many demonstrations of faith that everyone is familiar with. Moses had great faith to lead the people out of Egypt to a place where only God knew where they were going. In a strong statement of faith, imagine that Noah constructed a huge ship for over 100 years, but did it miles from water. Have faith in your students; have faith in yourself; have faith in God to help you through.

NOTES/THOUGHTS/PRAYERS

_____

_____

_____

_____

_____

_____

_____

_____

F

FORGIVENESS
(POWER OF)

Those with good sense are slow to anger,
and it is their glory to overlook an offense.

Proverbs 19:11 NRSV

When a teacher forgives a student for something, it is one of the most powerful things they can do. God encourages you to hand out forgiveness as a blessing to someone else, and in turn, a blessing to yourself.

NOTES/THOUGHTS/PRAYERS

_____

_____

_____

_____

_____

_____

_____

_____

F

FORGIVENESS
(WORKS)

Make allowance for each other's faults, and forgive anyone who offends you. Remember, the Lord forgave you, so you must forgive others.

Colossians 3:13 NLT

People make mistakes, and teachers are out there everyday to see them. You see them with children, parents, other teachers, and administration. But nobody's perfect, and it goes a long way to cut somebody some slack…just like God's gift to all of us.

F

NOTES/THOUGHTS/PRAYERS

_____

_____

_____

_____

_____

_____

_____

_____

F

FRIENDSHIP

There are "friends" who destroy each other, but a real friend sticks closer than a brother.

Proverbs 18:24 NLT

Teachers need close friends to help them through the everyday challenges with students, parents and the like. Give the gift of friendship to another teacher, and you will have a new "family" member.

NOTES/THOUGHTS/PRAYERS

_____

_____

_____

_____

_____

_____

_____

_____

_____

_____

G

GENEROSITY

"And I have been a constant example of how you can help those in need by working hard. You should remember the words of the Lord Jesus: 'It is more blessed to give than to receive.' "

Acts 20: 35 NLT

Perhaps, these famous words of Jesus are most commonly quoted during the Christmas season. But for teachers, this can apply every day. You have students in need, you work hard, and you give of yourself. Remember the opportunity to get God's blessing by giving, especially if being a teacher has become "just a job".

G

NOTES/THOUGHTS/PRAYERS

_____

_____

_____

_____

_____

_____

_____

_____

G

GENEROSITY
(GIVE A HELPING HAND)

Good people always lend freely to others,
and their children are a blessing.

Psalms 37: 26 NCV

Teachers know there are exceptions to this, but God has a gift for you in good parents to help out your classroom. Look for those that "lend freely" as they won't have a hidden agenda. You can probably find them through your favorite students.

G

NOTES/THOUGHTS/PRAYERS

_____

_____

_____

_____

_____

_____

_____

_____

_____

G

GENEROSITY
(RETURNS THE FAVOR)

"Give, and it will be given to you; good measure, pressed down, shaken together, running over, will be put into your lap. For the measure you give will be the measure you get back."

Luke 6:38 RSV

Teachers are constantly giving of themselves to their students. Luke's gospel quotes Christ to encourage you that in time, your generosity will be returned. What a great promise!

G

NOTES/THOUGHTS/PRAYERS

_____

_____

_____

_____

_____

_____

_____

_____

_____

G

GOSSIP
(CAN RUIN A SCHOOL)

As surely as a north wind brings rain,
so a gossiping tongue causes anger!

Proverbs 25:23 NLT

Gossip and backstabbing especially in schools can bring on a quick downward spiral. God's gift here is the reminder to stay out of it, and encourage others to do the same.

G

NOTES/THOUGHTS/PRAYERS

_____

_____

_____

_____

_____

_____

_____

_____

_____

G

GUILT
(MOVE ON FROM)

When they continued to ask Jesus their question, he raised up and said,
"Anyone here who has never sinned can throw the first stone at her."
Those who heard Jesus began to leave one by one, first the older men
and then the others.
Jesus was left there alone with the woman standing before him.
Jesus raised up again and asked her,
"Woman, where are they? Has no one judged you guilty?"
She answered, "No one, sir."
Then Jesus said, "I also don't judge you guilty. You may go now, but
don't sin anymore."

John 8:7, 9-11 NCV

With all the stuff that goes on in a teacher's day, there is likely to be something you are feeling guilty about. You may have made a mistake, or caused or contributed to an issue. It just comes with the territory, since you are constantly making decisions all the time about your class. The classic story recounted above basically says 1) nobody's perfect, 2) God is willing to forgive you, and 3) you should try not to make the same mistake again.

G

Notes/Thoughts/Prayers

_____

_____

_____

_____

_____

_____

_____

_____

_____

H

HAPPINESS
(KEEPS YOU GOING)

Worry weighs a person down; an encouraging word cheers a person up.

Proverbs 12:25 NLT

So even the expression "Don't worry, be happy" has biblical roots! God's gift of encouragement to another is one of the most valuable things he entrusts to teachers.

NOTES/THOUGHTS/PRAYERS

_____

_____

_____

_____

_____

_____

_____

H

HAPPINESS
(IS A GREAT REWARD)

What do people really get for all their hard work?
I have seen the burden God has placed
on us all. Yet God has made everything beautiful for its own time.
He has planted eternity in the human heart, but even so, people cannot
see the whole scope of God's work from beginning to end.
So I concluded there is nothing better than to be happy and enjoy
ourselves as long as we can.
And people should eat and drink and enjoy the fruits of their labor,
for these are gifts from God.

Ecclesiastes 3:9-13 NLT

Look again at the last sentence. Enjoy the gifts God has given you as a teacher. You deserve them.

NOTES/THOUGHTS/PRAYERS

_____

_____

_____

_____

_____

_____

_____

_____

HELPING HAND

Jesus answered, "As a man was going down from Jerusalem to
Jericho, some robbers attacked him.
They tore off his clothes, beat him,
and left him lying there, almost dead.
It happened that a priest was going down that road.
When he saw the man, he walked by on the other side.
Next, a Levite came there, and after he went over and looked at the
man, he walked by on the other side of the road.
Then a Samaritan traveling down the road came to where the hurt
man was. When he saw the man, he felt very sorry for him.
The Samaritan went to him, poured olive oil and wine on his
wounds, and bandaged them.
Then he put the hurt man on his own donkey and took him to an inn
where he cared for him. The next day, the Samaritan brought out two
coins, gave them to the innkeeper, and said,
'Take care of this man. If you spend more money on him, I will pay
it back to you when I come again.' "
Then Jesus said, "Which one of these three men do you think was a
neighbor to the man who was attacked by the robbers?"
The expert on the law answered, "The one who showed him mercy."

Luke 10:30-37 NCV

This is of course the famous story of the Good Samaritan as

told in the gospel of Luke. This passage is one of God's great gifts, with significant application for teachers. You might have that certain student that has been "beaten" down by the rigors of school, other teachers, mean students or the like. It comes with some risk to "invest" the time and caring to help these students, but it is the epitome of "Love Thy Neighbor", one of the most important tenets in life. Be on the look-out for chances to lend a helping hand, often not part of your regular job description.

Notes/Thoughts/Prayers

_____

_____

_____

_____

_____

_____

H

HONESTY
(BENEFITS OF)

Honesty guides good people; dishonesty destroys treacherous people.

Proverbs 11:3 NLT

Teachers have a complicated job. You deal with a lot of people – kids and parents in particular. Try to be as honest with your assessments and feedback as you can. These are a must for the benefit of the child and to help guide the parent. This isn't about so-called brutal honesty, which can be hurtful. Be guided by your caring attitude.

NOTES/THOUGHTS/PRAYERS

_____

_____

_____

_____

_____

_____

_____

_____

_____

H

HURT
(DON'T DWELL ON)

But Ruth replied, "Don't ask me to leave you and turn back. Wherever
you go, I will go; wherever you live, I will live.
Your people will be my people, and your God will be my God. Wherever
you die, I will die, and there I will be buried.
May the LORD punish me severely if I allow anything but death to
separate us!"

Ruth 1:16-17 NLT

The book of Ruth is the story of selfless devotion in
difficult times. We don't know if Ruth was a teacher or not.
But life had been rough for Ruth, her mother-in-law Naomi
and sister-in-law. All of their husbands had died, and life
was difficult for a widow thousands of years ago. Despite
deep pain though, Ruth had continued to show undying
support, love and kindness for her mother-in-law, Naomi.
Unfortunately, Naomi had responded to the circumstances
with bitterness. The example of a positive attitude when life
seems unfair is a gift from the bible. Things happen, but
you choose how to react.

H

NOTES/THOUGHTS/PRAYERS

_____

_____

_____

_____

_____

_____

_____

_____

I

INTEGRITY
(IS A GREAT MODEL)

When a man walks in integrity and justice,
happy are his children after him!

Proverbs 20:7 NABWRNT

Teachers don't just teach, but also are role models. 20-40 students at a time are watching your every move. Treat a student fairly, and the students respond.

I

NOTES/THOUGHTS/PRAYERS

_____

_____

_____

_____

_____

_____

_____

_____

_____

J

JOY
(FROM YOUR JOB)

You will enjoy the fruit of your labor.
How joyful and prosperous you will be!

Psalms 128: 2 NLT

Teachers are especially fortunate to receive this gift, but make sure you look for it. You have many occasions to see progress in your students through the results of your work. How great is that, since so many people may never get the same chance.

J

NOTES/THOUGHTS/PRAYERS

_____

_____

_____

_____

_____

_____

_____

_____

K

KINDNESS
(IS OFTEN RETURNED)

They answered, "Be kind to these people. If you please them and give them a kind answer, they will serve you always."

2 Chronicles 10:7 NCV

God gives the gift of kindness to the children through you. Kindness to all returns the favor.

K

NOTES/THOUGHTS/PRAYERS

_____

_____

_____

_____

_____

_____

_____

_____

K

KINDNESS
(HONEST)

When you talk, do not say harmful things, but say what people need—words that will help others become stronger. Then what you say will do good to those who listen to you.

Ephesians 4:29 NCV

You are possibly the closest non-family advisor your parents and students will ever have. They can sometimes hang on every word. God's reminder is to be straightforward, but not mean-spirited. This honest assessment helps them in the long run, although it can sometimes be unpleasant.

K

NOTES/THOUGHTS/PRAYERS

_____

_____

_____

_____

_____

_____

_____

_____

_____

K

KINDNESS

Do not neglect to show hospitality to strangers, for by doing that some have entertained angels without knowing it.

Hebrews 13:2 NRSV

The movie "Pay It Forward" was a great example of doing good deeds in advance. These good deeds can make a difference in someone's life in the future. Your "little angels" could be the next to make a difference in someone's life if you create the right environment in theirs.

K

NOTES/THOUGHTS/PRAYERS

_____

_____

_____

_____

_____

_____

_____

_____

K

KINDNESS

God blesses those who are merciful, for they will be shown mercy.

Matthew 5:7 NLT

Kids mess up. Parents make mistakes. Harsh words are said. Be the first to show forgiveness and it will be returned so you can move on.

NOTES/THOUGHTS/PRAYERS

_____

_____

_____

_____

_____

_____

_____

_____

L

LAUGHTER
(DON'T FORGET THE)

We laughed, we sang, we couldn't believe our good fortune. We were the
talk of the nations – "God was wonderful to them!"
God was wonderful to us;
we are one happy people. And now, God, do it again – bring rains to our
drought-stricken lives, So those who planted their crops in despair will
shout hurrahs at the harvest,
So those who went off with heavy hearts will come home laughing, with
armloads of blessing.

Psalm 126: 2-6 Message

Don't forget to celebrate and have a little fun, especially after a period of difficulty.

NOTES/THOUGHTS/PRAYERS

_____

_____

_____

_____

_____

_____

_____

_____

_____

L

LAUGHTER
(KEEPS SPIRITS UP)

A happy heart is like good medicine,
but a broken spirit drains your strength.

Proverbs 17:22 NCV

A happy heart is an old expression for laughter and merriment. A cheerful disposition really works wonders on both you and the people around you. Enjoy your day! Don't let the "Eeyores" of the world get you down.

L

NOTES/THOUGHTS/PRAYERS

_____

_____

_____

_____

_____

_____

_____

_____

L

LEADERSHIP

Love and truth form a good leader;
sound leadership is formed on loving integrity.

Proverbs 20:27 Message

Perhaps as much as anything, young families look up to teachers as leaders. As a leader, accept this guidance as a gift from God.

NOTES/THOUGHTS/PRAYERS

_____

_____

_____

_____

_____

_____

_____

_____

_____

L

LISTENING

The Lord said to Moses, "Why do you cry to me? Tell the people of Israel to go forward. Lift up your rod, and stretch out your hand over the sea and divide it, that the people of Israel may go on dry ground through the sea." Then Moses stretched out his hand over the sea; and the Lord drove the sea back by a strong east wind all night, and made the sea dry land, and the waters were divided. And the people of Israel went into the midst of the sea on dry ground, the waters being a wall to them on their right hand and on their left.

Exodus 14:15-16, 21-22 RSV

There is no better listener in the bible than Moses. He was personally in charge of saving God's chosen people, the Israelites, from the oppression of the Egyptians. Exodus is full of commands from God, followed precisely and with great courage by Moses. The parting of the Red Sea is perhaps the greatest feat of listening ever. (You can imagine that Moses was not exactly sure what he heard when God said walk into the ocean!) Perhaps, one of your students has something to say and no-one to say it to. Just a simple act of listening can be your gift to someone.

NOTES/THOUGHTS/PRAYERS

_____

_____

_____

_____

_____

_____

_____

_____

L

LOVE

Don't just pretend to love others. Really love them. Hate what is wrong.
Hold tightly to what is good.

Romans 12:9 NLT

Loving a student really means never giving up on them and constantly expressing hope. Show them you value the difference between right and wrong, something they can hold onto for their whole life.

L

NOTES/THOUGHTS/PRAYERS

_____

_____

_____

_____

_____

_____

_____

_____

L

LOVE

Like a cool drink of water when you're worn out and weary,
is a letter from a long lost friend.

Proverbs 25:25 Message

You know how much a letter or phone call from an old friend means. From your student's perspective, that "lost" friend could be his or her teacher, from whose graces they may have fallen some time ago. So too God reminds teachers of the gift of a kind or encouraging note to struggling student, and how much this can mean.

NOTES/THOUGHTS/PRAYERS

L

LOVE

Love is patient and kind.
Love is not jealous or boastful or proud or rude.
It does not demand its own way.
It is not irritable, and it keeps no record of being wronged.
It does not rejoice about injustice
but rejoices whenever the truth wins out.
Love never gives up, never loses faith, is always hopeful, and endures
through every circumstance.

1 Corinthians 13:4-8 NLT

We often hear this at weddings, but teachers can receive some great blessings when they show love to their students. What does it mean to love one another? God is giving us a checklist here of what love means, which you can apply even to those students who aren't so "lovable".

L

Notes/Thoughts/Prayers

_____

_____

_____

_____

_____

_____

_____

_____

_____

_____

M

MERCY
(RETURNS THE FAVOR)

God blesses those who are merciful, for they will be shown mercy.

Matthew 5:7 NLT

What a great concept. Give a kid a break, and pick up a little mercy for yourself. Now that's a gift from God.

Notes/Thoughts/Prayers

_____

_____

_____

_____

_____

_____

_____

_____

M

MONEY

Fierce troubles came down on the people of those churches,
pushing them to the very limit.
The trial exposed their true colors:
They were incredibly happy, though desperately poor.
The pressure triggered something totally unexpected: an outpouring of
pure and generous gifts. I was there and saw it for myself.

2 Corinthians 8:2-3 Message

Teachers don't do it for the money! And they put up with a lot! The leader of the Christian movement Paul provides this inspirational passage from centuries ago about the people of the Christian church in Macedonia. Despite their trials and lack of money, they were extremely generous with their gifts. God must have also had teachers in mind, because they know that it doesn't take money to be fulfilled.

M

NOTES/THOUGHTS/PRAYERS

P

PATIENCE
(CAN TAKE A WHILE!)

"And I will bless her and give you a son from her! Yes, I will bless her richly, and she will become the mother of many nations. Kings of nations will be among her descendants." Then Abraham bowed down to the ground, but he laughed to himself in disbelief. "How could I become a father at the age of 100?" he thought. "And how can Sarah have a baby when she is ninety years old?"

Genesis 17:16-17 NLT

The Bible has many examples of patience, but perhaps this story about Abraham is one of the most unusual. Abraham, one of the key figures in the first book of the Bible, received a promise from God that he and his descendants would be the leaders of the Jewish nation, a bloodline that ultimately led to Jesus Christ. The problem was that at 75, he didn't have any kids! 25 years later, God re-confirmed his promise to give him many descendants, and Abraham did become that great leader. Students can also benefit from your patience with them.

P

NOTES/THOUGHTS/PRAYERS

_____

_____

_____

_____

_____

_____

_____

_____

_____

P

PERCEPTION

Yes, just as you can identify a tree by its fruit,
so you can identify people by their actions.

Matthew 7:20 NLT

A teacher has to make a lot of assessments about the people they interact with – parents, children, administration and the like. God provides some hints about how to get past the surface to assess those you are around. More than other characteristics, it is the quality of the fruit that is the most important determinant in the quality of the tree. Similarly, it is the actions of the people that most identify their character.

P

NOTES/THOUGHTS/PRAYERS

_____

_____

_____

_____

_____

_____

_____

P

PERCEPTION
(CAN SERVE YOU WELL)

Do not be deceived: "Bad company ruins good morals."

1 Corinthians 15:33 NRSV

A school consists of a lot of different people: parents, students, administration, teachers, school board, etc. God's gift to us through author Paul applies in so many circumstances in this dynamic environment. Be aware that it does apply! When you see good morals slipping in your school or class, identify how strong the influence of a "bad apple" or two may be in causing the situation, and take action accordingly.

P

NOTES/THOUGHTS/PRAYERS

_____

_____

_____

_____

_____

_____

_____

_____

_____

P

PERCEPTION

Don't jump to conclusions –
there may be a perfectly good explanation for what you just saw.

Proverbs 25:8 Message

Teachers need to go with their gut instinct every day, especially in their role as judge and jury in "who did what to who" on the playground. You need those instincts, but God's gift of wisdom here is to keep a gut check in mind.

P

NOTES/THOUGHTS/PRAYERS

P

PERSEVERANCE

So let us not grow weary in doing what is right,
for we will reap at harvest time, if we do not give up.

Galatians 6:9 NABWRNT

Listen to God's encouragement. Stay your right course. Don't give up. You might be frustrated though because "harvest time" does not go by the school calendar or by grade. It may take years to get the desired result, and you might never see the "fruit" of a student finally making that break-through. But it will be there.

P

NOTES/THOUGHTS/PRAYERS

P

PERSEVERANCE
(BUILDS CHARACTER)

We also have joy with our troubles,
because we know that these troubles produce patience.
And patience produces character, and character produces hope.

Romans 5:3-4 NCV

This is not what you expected, but is one of the great gifts from God. Get this – your troubles are a character builder! You know there are bad days for teachers. You can be encouraged that these are not a punishment, but rather helping to produce a base of hope for the future.

P

NOTES/THOUGHTS/PRAYERS

_____

_____

_____

_____

_____

_____

_____

_____

_____

P

PERSEVERANCE
(SHOWS PRINCIPLE)

Since he himself has gone through suffering and testing,
he is able to help us when we are being tested.

Hebrews 2:18 NLT

This passage refers to the tremendous suffering Christ went through during his life and ultimately before his death. Who better to receive encouragement from, than the one who experienced the greatest suffering ever recorded? His gifts in this area are throughout the bible. Keep to your principles, even if there is some discomfort along the way.

P

NOTES/THOUGHTS/PRAYERS

_____

_____

_____

_____

_____

_____

_____

_____

_____

P

PERSONAL GIFTS

God works in different ways,
but it is the same God who does the work in all of us.

1 Corinthians 12:6 NLT

God is working in all of us, but he works differently in
different people. He has given everyone gifts to use in this
life. For you, he gave you the gift of teaching and maybe
even some others that you may know now or find out later.
For others, it may be a different gift. Use the gifts he has
given you to bless others.

P

NOTES/THOUGHTS/PRAYERS

_____

_____

_____

_____

_____

_____

_____

_____

P

PERSONAL GIFTS

"Now they know that everything you gave me comes from you."

John 17:7 NCV

In this passage, even Jesus acknowledges that his many gifts came from the father. Don't waste your special talents and interests, because God gave them to you for a reason. Continue to strive to seek those talents out and make the most of them. Get a little better every day in every way.

P

NOTES/THOUGHTS/PRAYERS

_____

_____

_____

_____

_____

_____

_____

_____

P

POSITIVE THINKING

And now, dear brothers and sisters, one final thing.
Fix your thoughts on what is true,
and honorable, and right, and pure, and lovely, and admirable.
Think about things that are excellent and worthy of praise.

Philippians 4:8 NLT

So now you know – it's not the self help gurus of the 20th century that came up with the power of positive thinking! In fact, Paul speaks to the issue 2000 years ago. In this letter directed to the Christian church in Philippi, it is noteworthy that he is providing this encouragement from jail (on trumped up charges)! The days for teachers are often long and challenging and it would be easy to get down. Keep your mind on the good things in life to keep your spirits up.

P

NOTES/THOUGHTS/PRAYERS

_____

_____

_____

_____

_____

_____

_____

_____

_____

P

PRIORITIES

Then he put a little child among them. Taking the child in his arms, he said to them, "Anyone who welcomes a little child like this on my behalf welcomes me, and anyone who welcomes me welcomes not only me, but also my Father who sent me."

Mark 9:36-37 NLT

Then Jesus called for the children and said to the disciples, "Let the children come to me. Don't stop them! For the Kingdom of God belongs to those who are like these children."

Luke 18:16 NLT

Your choice of a career as a teacher is a blessing. Children had a high place in the Christ's priorities, and they obviously do in yours too.

P

NOTES/THOUGHTS/PRAYERS

_____

_____

_____

_____

_____

_____

_____

_____

_____

P

Priorities

Children are a gift from the Lord; they are a reward from him.

Psalms 127:3 NLT

In the days of Jesus, the world had a much different view of children, which was nowhere near the level of importance we hold them in today. Christ changed that view. How great is it that you are involved in the upbringing of these students. What a gift from God!

P

NOTES/THOUGHTS/PRAYERS

_____

_____

_____

_____

_____

_____

_____

_____

R

REST
(GET SOME)

And on the seventh day God ended his work which he had made; and he rested on the seventh day from all his work which he had made.

Genesis 2:2 NKJV

Then Jesus said, "Let's go off by ourselves to a quiet place and rest awhile." He said this because there were so many people coming and going that Jesus and his apostles didn't even have time to eat.

Mark 6:31 NLT

Enjoy the weekends. Recharge during the holidays and summer. In these passages, God reminds us that he himself even needed some rest.

R

NOTES/THOUGHTS/PRAYERS

_____

_____

_____

_____

_____

_____

_____

_____

_____

_____

R

RISK
(TAKE SOME)

*Those who wait for perfect weather will never plant seeds; those who
look at every cloud will never harvest crops.*

Ecclesiastes 11:4 NCV

Teachers can operate "by the book", but often need to go
"out on a limb". God reminds that sometimes there is no
perfect time, but you just need to go for it. If you don't, the
harvest might never come in.

R

Notes/Thoughts/Prayers

_____

_____

_____

_____

_____

_____

_____

_____

S

SERVICE
(CHRIST REDEFINES)

Jesus called them together and said, "The other nations have rulers.
You know that those rulers love to show their power over the people, and
their important leaders love to use all their authority.
But it should not be that way among you. Whoever wants to become great
among you must serve the rest of you like a servant.
Whoever wants to become the first among you must serve all of you like a
slave. In the same way, the Son of Man did not come to be served. He
came to serve others and to give his life as a ransom for many people."

Mark 10:42-45 NCV

Christ modeled the gift of servanthood to the world. He caught the world by surprise. Everyone expected a great powerful king and ruler for the coming of the son of God. Instead, he turned the world upside down and served people instead. In your leadership role as a teacher, you will be most successful when you serve your students.

S

NOTES/THOUGHTS/PRAYERS

_____

_____

_____

_____

_____

_____

_____

_____

S

SERVICE
(FOR ALL)

Later, Matthew invited Jesus and his disciples to his home as dinner guests, along with many tax collectors and other disreputable sinners. But when the Pharisees saw this, they asked his disciples, "Why does your teacher eat with such scum?" When Jesus heard this, he said, "Healthy people don't need a doctor—sick people do."

Mathew 9: 10-12 NLT

God has put you in with kids where learning comes easy, and those where progress is much more difficult. Teachers can easily gravitate to the advanced students. Just as the sick people need a doctor more than healthy ones, so too the slower child needs a teacher more than the advanced kid. By spending some more time where it is needed, you are acknowledging God's gift as modeled by Jesus. No question however that this is easier said than done.

S

Notes/Thoughts/Prayers

_____

_____

_____

_____

_____

_____

_____

_____

_____

S

STRENGTH

*We pray that you'll have the strength to stick it out over the long haul –
not the grim strength of gritting your teeth but the glory-strength God
gives. It is strength that endures the unendurable, and spills over into joy,
thanking the Father who makes us strong enough to take part in
everything bright and beautiful he has for us.*

Colossians 1:11-12 Message

Teachers need to reach back all the time to pull out the strength to finish the day, or the week, or the school year. The Message has a unique way of differentiating the gut-it-out effort, and the strength that comes from the joy of knowing the impact you are having on these young lives. We pray for all teachers to get this latter strength.

S

NOTES/THOUGHTS/PRAYERS

_____

_____

_____

_____

_____

_____

_____

_____

_____

_____

T

TEAMWORK
(IMPROVES SUCCESS)

The human body has many parts, but the many parts make up one whole body. So it is with the body of Christ. But our bodies have many parts, and God has put each part just where he wants it. If one part suffers, all the parts suffer with it, and if one part is honored, all the parts are glad. All of you together are Christ's body, and each of you is a part of it.

1 Corinthians 12:12,18, 26-27 NLT

God points out to teachers the wisdom of teamwork. Even a great teacher recognizes that they are only part of a student's life, and to the best of their ability, must recognize the importance of the rest of the parts of the "body" (parents, siblings, friends, other teachers, administration, coaches, etc.) to the student's highest achievement.

T

Notes/Thoughts/Prayers

T

TENDERNESS

Brothers and sisters, we urge you to warn those who are lazy. Encourage those who are timid. Take tender care of those who are weak. Be patient with everyone.

1 Thessalonians 5:14 NLT

This passage is a beautiful reminder of the soft side of being a teacher. During a hectic day in the classroom, this is easier said than done. But God reminds us to always try with those who need that tender or patient touch.

T

NOTES/THOUGHTS/PRAYERS

WISDOM
(DEMONSTRATING YOUR)

Direct your children onto the right path, and when they are older,
they will not leave it.

Proverbs 22:6 NLT

The wisdom of Solomon, author of this proverb, is evident. Elementary school teachers are so important in helping to set students on the right path for their whole life. Consider your advice and counsel carefully.

NOTES/THOUGHTS/PRAYERS

WISDOM
(BETTER THAN MONEY)

Joyful is the person who finds wisdom, the one who gains understanding. For wisdom is more profitable than silver, and her wages are better than gold. Wisdom is more precious than rubies; nothing you desire can compare with her. She offers you long life in her right hand, and riches and honor in her left. She will guide you down delightful paths; all her ways are satisfying. Wisdom is a tree of life to those who embrace her; happy are those who hold her tightly.

Proverbs 3:13-18 NLT

Teachers are at the core of implementing these words of King Solomon. Knowledge is better than money and things, and should be at the top of the list of desires.

NOTES/THOUGHTS/PRAYERS

WISDOM
(BETTER THAN MUSCLE)

It's better to be wise than strong; intelligence outranks muscle any day.

Proverbs 24:21 Message

God has a gift for your students too. Pass it on!

Notes/Thoughts/Prayers

_____

_____

_____

_____

_____

_____

_____

_____

_____

WORRY
(DOESN'T ADD MUCH)

Can all your worries add a single moment to your life? And if worry can't accomplish a little thing like that, what's the use of worrying over bigger things?

Luke 12:25-26 NLT

God knows teachers can have a lot to worry about. Every day, new challenges are thrown in their directions whether it is children, parents, administration. But here Luke quotes Christ, who reminds us that since worry can't add a moment to your life, take a different approach and relax a little from your day to day worries.

NOTES/THOUGHTS/PRAYERS

_____

_____

_____

_____

_____

_____

_____

_____

WORRY
(DON'T)

Worry weighs us down; a cheerful word picks us up.

Proverbs 12:25 Message

You know that kid, the one with the weight of the world on his shoulders. A cheerful word from the teacher has a great chance of making a difference in his day… or even his life.

Notes/Thoughts/Prayers

_____

_____

_____

_____

_____

_____

_____

_____

_____

Y

YOUR GIFTS

In his grace, God has given us different gifts for doing certain things well. So if God has given you the ability to prophesy, speak out with as much faith as God has given you.
If your gift is serving others, serve them well.
If you are a teacher, teach well.
If your gift is to encourage others, be encouraging.
If it is giving, give generously.
If God has given you leadership ability, take the responsibility seriously.
And if you have a gift for showing kindness to others, do it gladly.

Romans 12:6-8 NLT

If you are a teacher, God has given you *all* these gifts. You are truly benefiting from God's glory.

Y

Notes/Thoughts/Prayers

_____

_____

_____

_____

_____

_____

_____

_____

_____

GOD'S GREATEST GIFTS

But the Spirit produces the fruit of love, joy, peace, patience, kindness, goodness, faithfulness, gentleness, self-control. There is no law that says these things are wrong.

Galatians 5:22-23 NCV

This is perhaps my favorite passage, because it lays out all the gifts God promises for us in life. You have to let the Holy Spirit work in you to receive these things. What a great list! Who wouldn't want the quality of life contained in these great promises?

SOME FINAL THOUGHTS

I'm hopeful that these comments have made sense to you, and you can see some of the gifts God has made available for teachers. There are hundreds and thousands of other segments of the bible that can apply to you as you go about your day. In a confusing society of moral relativism, teachers can also benefit from the core values re-enforced over and over again in the bible. These are all a manifestation of God's love for us.

Remember:

Nothing can separate us from God's love.
What shall we say about such wonderful things as these?
If God is for us, who can ever be against us?

Romans 8:31 NLT

R

References

References marked with **RSV** are from *The Revised Standard Version*. 1971. Logos Research Systems, Inc.: Oak Harbor, WA

References marked with **KJV** are from *The Holy Bible: King James Version*. 1995 (electronic ed. of the 1769 edition of the 1611 Authorized Version.). Logos Research Systems, Inc.: Bellingham WA

Scripture readings marked with **NABWRNT** are taken from the New American Bible With Revised New Testament Copyright 1986 Confraternity of Christian Doctrine, Washington, D.C. All Rights Reserved.

The Scripture quotations contained herein are from the **NRSV** are the New Revised Standard Version Bible, Copyright © 1989, Division of Christian Education of the National Council of the Churches of Christ in the U.S.A., and are used by permission. All rights reserved. Thomas Nelson Publishers: Nashville

Scriptures quoted from **NCV** are from *The Holy Bible: New Century Version*®, copyright © 2005 by Thomas Nelson, Inc. Used by permission.

Scripture taken from the **NKJV** are from New King James Version. Copyright 1979, 1980, 1982 by Thomas Nelson, Inc. Used by permission. All rights reserved.

R

CPSIA information can be obtained
at www.ICGtesting.com
Printed in the USA
LVHW090750160122
708692LV00014B/170